Biff and Chip had hoppers.

Biff and Chip set off.

The red hopper was big.

Dad got on it.

Dad and Kipper set off.

Pop!

Wilma had a kitten.

Catkin ran off.

Wilma had lost Catkin.

She was not on the bed.

She was not in the bin.

She was not in the bag.

But she was in the basket.

Wilma put a bell on Catkin.

Mum and Kipper went
shopping.

Kipper got the trolley.

Mum put cans in the trolley.

She put bags in the trolley.

Kipper put a big egg in the trolley.

Mum did not see the
big egg.

Mum saw the big egg.

Kipper had to put the egg
back.

Kipper had a caterpillar.

Kipper put the caterpillar
in a box.

He put leaves in the box.

Then it was not a
caterpillar.

It was a chrysalis.

But it was not a chrysalis.

It was a butterfly.

Chip got a crab.

Dad put it in the bucket.

They got lots of crabs.

Then Biff got an enormous crab.

Dad held the enormous crab.

The crabs got out.

Did the enormous crab
nip Dad?

No! It did not.

Wilma and Wilf had a trampoline.

Dad put the net up.

Wilma got on. She went up and down.

Wilf got on. Up and down he went.

Dad got on the trampoline.

Up he went . . .

. . . but not down.